HOLY FAMILY SCHOOL

MUSICANADA 2

Phyllis Schafer
Senior Author

Yvette Stack

HOLT, RINEHART AND WINSTON OF CANADA, LIMITED, TORONTO

MUSICANADA 2

Phyllis Schafer

Yvette Stack

ISBN 0-03-922214-4

Project Editor Katharine Vanderlinden
Permissions Editor Diane Robitaille
Art Director Many Pens Design
Cover Illustration Terry Shoffner
Illustrators
Carlos Freire
Vesna Krstanovich
Loris Lesynski
Louise Phillips

Canadian Cataloguing in Publication Data
Schafer, Phyllis
Musicanada 2. Student book

ISBN 0-03-922214-4

1. Music–Manuals, text-books, etc.
2. Music–Theory, Elementary–Juvenile literature.
I. Stack, Yvette. II. Title.

MT930.S36 1991   781   C90-093213-9

Printed in Canada   1 2 3 4 5 94 93 92 91 90

CONTENTS

AUTUMN

WINTER

SPRING

AUTUMN

TO EVERYONE IN ALL THE WORLD

Traditional

To everyone in all the world

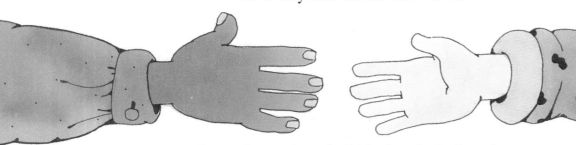

I reach my hand, I shake their hand.

To everyone in all the world

I shake my hand like this.

All,   all   to - geth - er,

The whole wide world around,

I   may not know their   lin - go,

But I can say "By jingo!

No   mat - ter where you   live,

We can shake hands."

LISTENING:

"Hélène's Dance"

French Canadian

Make the sounds of the beat.

  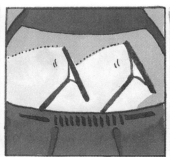 

Tap the beat as you listen to "Hélène's Dance."

JOSIE DANCE

Music Traditional/Words by Jos Wuytack

2. Yes, we know the Josie dance, the Josie dance, the Josie dance.
Yes, we know the Josie dance, the Josie dance from France.

3. Let's all do the Josie dance, the Josie dance, the Josie dance.
Let's all do the Josie dance, the Josie dance from France.

THE THREE BILLY GOATS GRUFF

Traditional

Listen to the story. Play the instruments.

SEESAW SACRADOWN (1)

Traditional

Find the high, middle, low sounds.

saw,

way to

See-

sac-ra-

Which is the

Lon - don

down,

Town?

up and

way to

One foot

one foot

This is the

Lon - don Town.

down,

Play the song. Use these bells.

C F C

SEE THE LITTLE DUCKLINGS

German Folk Song

Tap the melody as you sing. Where does the melody go up?
Where does it go down? Where does it stay the same?

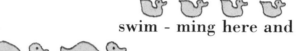
swim - ming here and

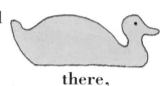
there,

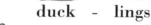
duck - lings

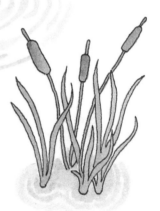

tle

lit-

the

See

Heads down in the

wa - ter,

tails up in the
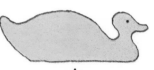

air.

LISTEN TO THE WATER

Bob Schneider

Follow the melody as you sing.

Chorus

Lis - ten to the wa - ter, Lis - ten to the wa - ter,

Roll - ing down the riv - er.

Lis - ten to the wa - ter, Lis - ten to the wa - ter,

Roll - ing down the riv - er.

Verse

1. We saw some 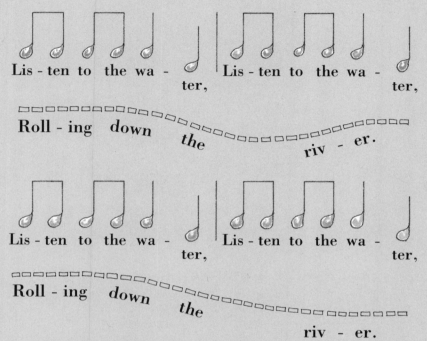 by the waterside,

Saw some by the waterside,

We saw some by the waterside,

Oh, Oh,

oh by the oh by the

wa - ter - side, wa - ter - side.

2. 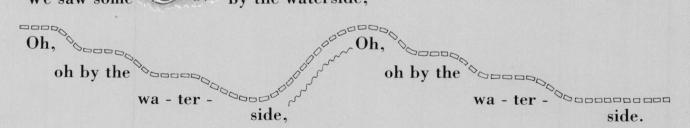 3. 4.

LISTENING:

As you listen to the music, follow the path of each fish with your finger.
Which paths are longer?

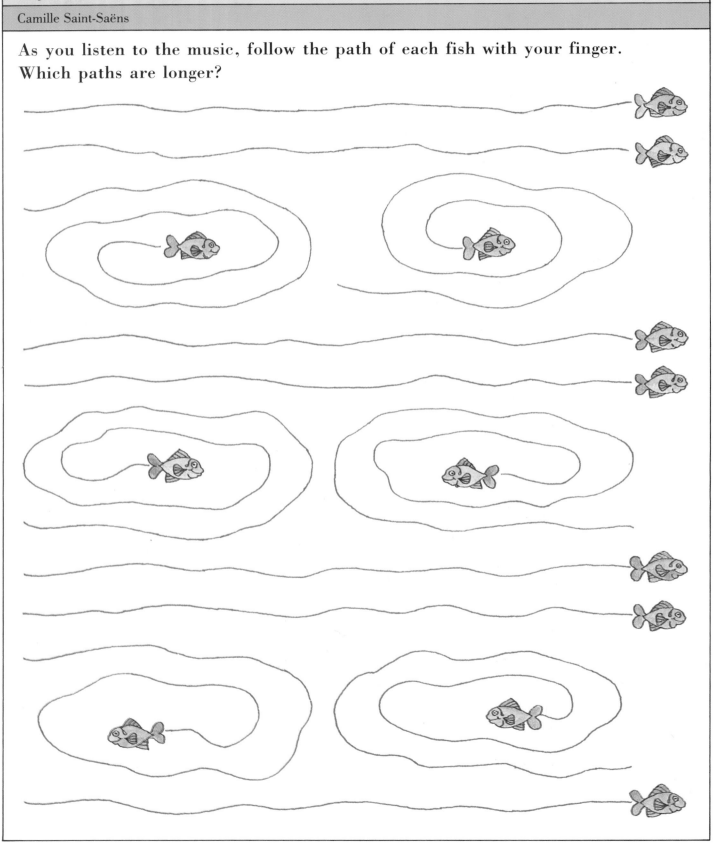

Can you hear these instruments?
They are all members of the String Family. How are they played?

SALLY, SALLY, HOW ARE YOU?

Traditional

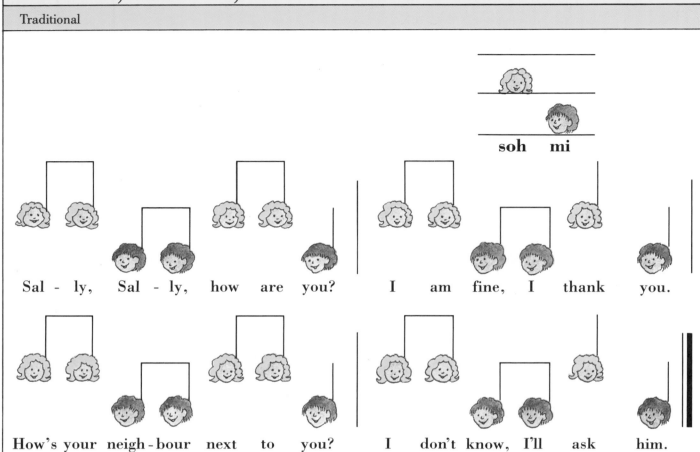

soh   mi

Sal - ly, Sal - ly, how are you?   I   am   fine, I   thank   you.

How's your neigh-bour next to you?   I don't know, I'll   ask   him.

ENGINE, ENGINE NUMBER NINE

Traditional

En - gine, en - gine num - ber nine, go - ing down the CN line.

If the train goes off the track, will I get my mon - ey back?

Yes, you will. Thank you.

OLIVER TWIST

Traditional

Follow the bouncing ball as you sing.

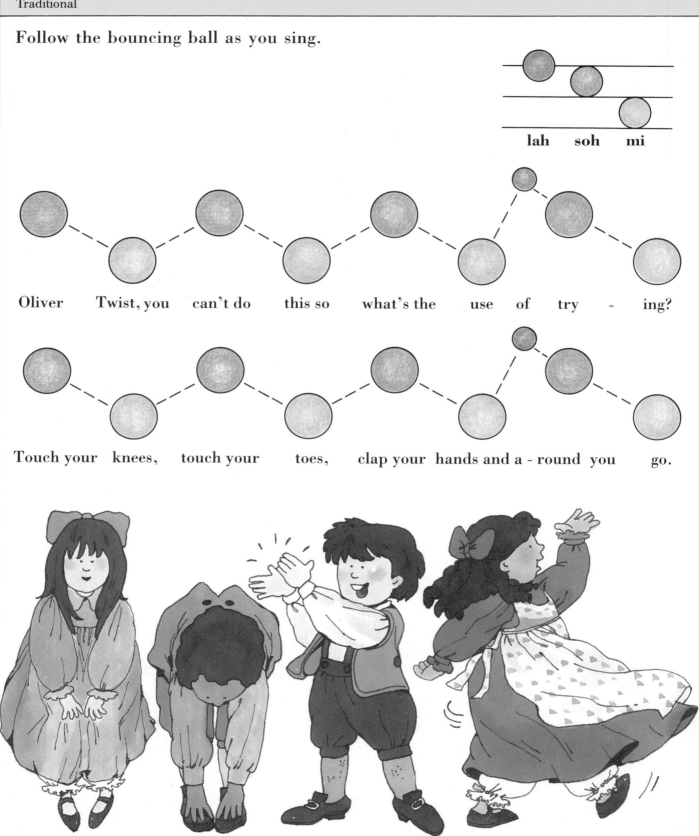

lah   soh   mi

Oliver   Twist, you   can't do   this so   what's the   use   of   try   -   ing?

Touch your   knees,   touch your   toes,   clap your   hands and a - round   you   go.

THANKS A LOT

Raffi

This is the house where the notes live. Follow the notes as you sing.

1. Thanks a lot, Thanks a lot,

Thanks for the sun in the sky.

Thanks a lot, Thanks a lot,

Thanks for the clouds so—— high. ——

2. Thanks a lot, thanks a lot,
Thanks for the whispering wind.
Thanks a lot, thanks a lot,
Thanks for the birds in the spring.

3. Thanks a lot, thanks a lot
Thanks for the moonlit night.
Thanks a lot, thanks a lot,
Thanks for the stars so bright.

HERE WE COME

Phyllis Schafer

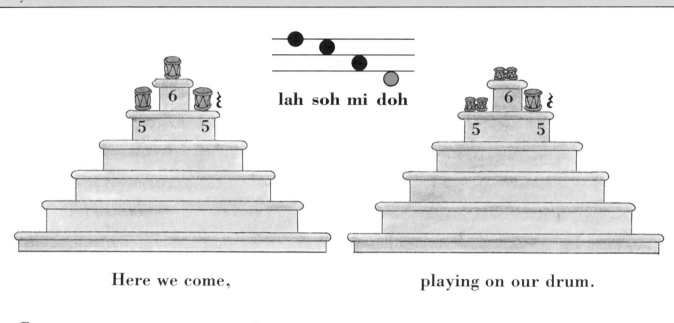

lah soh mi doh

Here we come,

playing on our drum.

Boom di-di,

boom di-di,

rum tum tum!

This is the **doh** finder. ⊫ It tells us where to find the **doh** notes.

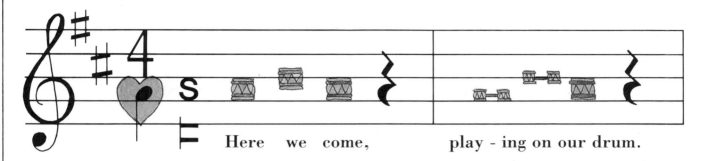

Here we come, play - ing on our drum.

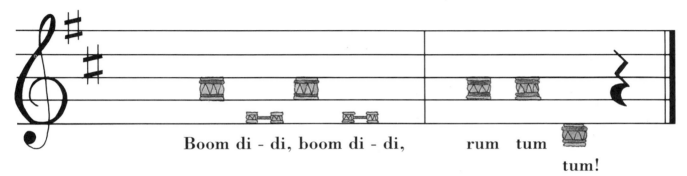

Boom di - di, boom di - di, rum tum tum!

⊫ tells you where **doh** lives. Name the note that begins the song.

MR. MONDAY

Traditional

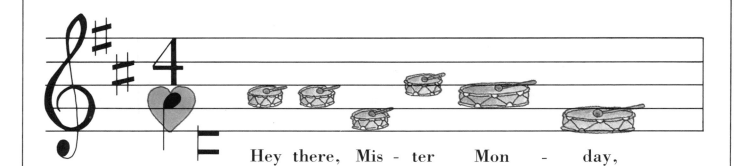

Hey there, Mis - ter   Mon - day,

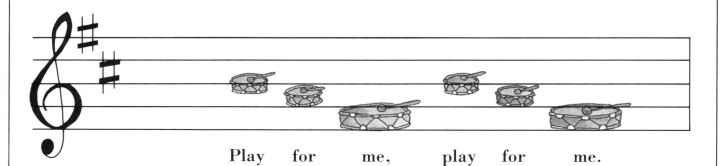

Play   for   me,   play   for   me.

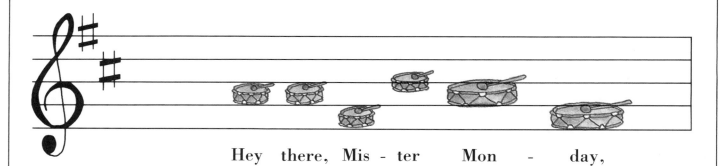

Hey   there, Mis - ter   Mon - day,

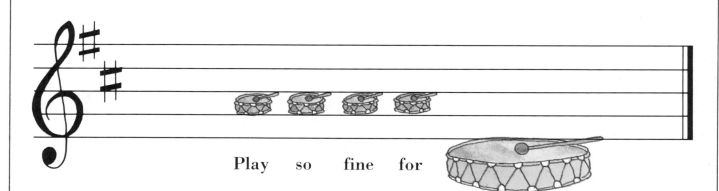

Play   so   fine   for

me.

Play these rhythms for the days of the week. Play each rhythm four times.

Mr. Monday

Mr. Tuesday

Mr. Wednesday

Mr. Thursday

Mr. Friday

Mr. Saturday

Mr. Sunday

THE GRAND OLD DUKE OF YORK

Maureen Raffey and Bernard Lodge

1.Oh, the grand old Duke of York,
He had ten thousand men.

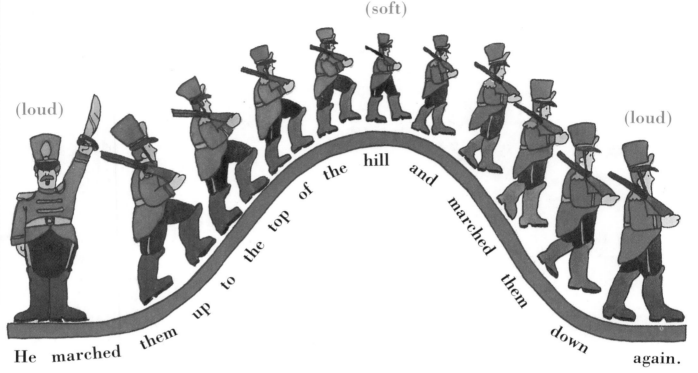

(soft)

(loud)

(loud)

He marched them up to the top of the hill and marched them down again.

Now, when they were up they were up,
And when they were down they were down,
And when they were only halfway up,
They were neither up nor down.

2. The grand old Duke of York,
His men were half asleep,
He marched them through a river,
But the river was too deep.
And some of them did splash,
And some of them did swim,
And some did soundly shake his hand
And bid farewell to him.

(slow)

(fast)

3. The grand old Duke of York,
He found himself alone.
He sat right down on the top of a drum
And there did weep and moan.

His men they all were lost,
His horse away had run.
He only wished that all his travels
Never had begun.

4. The grand old Duke of York,
He heard a bugle sound.
He jumped right up and looked about,
His heart began to pound.

He saw them in rows of five,
He saw them in rows of ten,
And they all lined up in front of him
Till he had ten thousand men.

THIS IS HALLOWE'EN

Poem

Dorothy Brown Thompson

Use low, middle, high sounds to tell a Hallowe'en story.

Goblins on the doorstep,
Phantoms in the air,
Owls on witches' gateposts
Giving stare for stare.

Cats on flying broomsticks,
Bats against the moon,
Stirrings round of fate-cakes
With a solemn spoon.

Whirling apple parings,
Figures draped in sheets

Dodging, disappearing
Up and down the streets.

Jack-o'-lanterns grinning,
Shadows on the screen,

Shrieks and starts and laughter—
This is Hallowe'en!

STRANGE HALLOWE'EN

Eunice Boardman

Tap the melody as you listen.

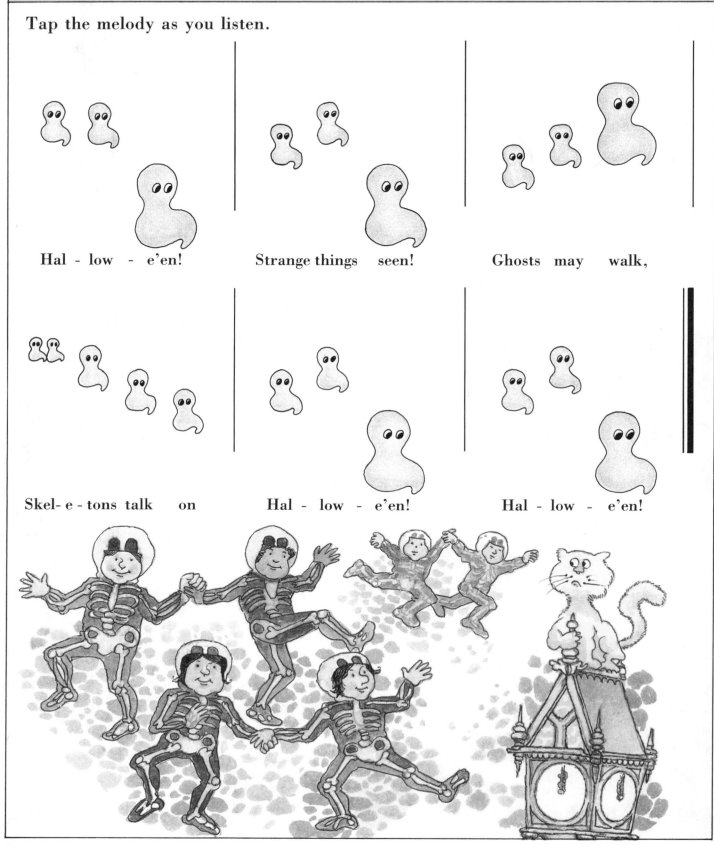

Hal - low - e'en!   Strange things   seen!   Ghosts   may   walk,

Skel- e -tons talk   on   Hal - low - e'en!   Hal - low - e'en!

24

PASS THE WITCH'S BROOMSTICK

Game Song

Pass the witch's broomstick round and round the room.

When the music's playing, quickly pass the broom.

Anyone is out if the broomstick drops,

Or the one who has it when the music stops.

THREE LITTLE FISHES

Saxie Dowell

Verse

Down in the mead-ow in a lit - tle bit - ty pool, swam

three lit - tle fish - ies and a ma - ma fish - ie too.

"Swim!" said the ma - ma fish - ie, "Swim if you can." And they

swam and they swam all o - ver the dam.

Chorus

Boop   boop   dit - tem dat - tem   what - tem   chu!

Boop   boop   dit - tem dat - tem   what - tem   chu!

Boop   boop   dit - tem dat - tem   what - tem   chu!   And they

swam   and they   swam   all   o - ver   the   dam.

27

TIDEO

Traditional

Play a game of sound and silence. Find all the silent beats and sing them in your thoughts. Sing the rest of the song out loud.

1. Pass one win - dow ti - de - o, Pass two win - dows ti - de - o.

Pass three win - dows ti - de - o, Jin - gle at the win - dows ti - de - o.

Jin - glin' Jin - glin', Jing - a - lin' Joe, Jin - gle at the win - dows ti - de - o.

(Sing this line two times)

2. Pass one win - dow ti - de Pass two win - dows ti - de

Pass three win - dows ti - de Jin - gle at the win - dows ti - de

Jin - glin' Jin - glin', Jing - a - lin' Joe, Jin - gle at the win - dows ti - de

(Sing this line two times)

28

3. Pass one win - dow ti   Pass two win - dows ti

Pass three win - dows ti   Jin-gle at the win -dows ti

Jin-glin' Jin-glin', Jing - a - lin' Joe,   Jin-gle at the win -dows ti

(Sing this line two times)

4. Pass one win - dow   Pass two win - dows

Pass three win - dows   Jin-gle at the win -dows

Jin-glin' Jin-glin', Jing - a - lin' Joe,   Jin-gle at the win -dows

(Sing this line two times)

29

PAWPAW PATCH

Game Song

1. Where, oh, where is pret - ty lit - tle El - lie,

Where, oh, where is pret - ty lit - tle El - lie,

Where, oh, where is pret - ty lit - tle El - lie,

Way down yon-der in the paw - paw patch.

2. Pickin' up pawpaws, put 'em in a basket...

3. Come on boys, let's go find her...

"Peel the Orange"

"Through the Wicket"

BOUGHT ME A CAT

Traditional

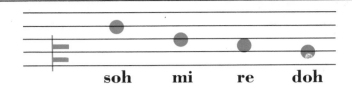

soh   mi   re   doh

1. Bought me a   cat,   cat   pleased   me,

Fed   my   cat   un - der   yon - der   tree.

Cat   went   fid - dle - i -   fee,   fid - dle - i -   fee.

2. Bought me a hen, hen pleased me,
Fed my hen under yonder tree.

Hen went

chip - sy,   chop - sy,

Cat went fiddle-i-fee, fiddle-i-fee.

3. Bought me a duck, duck pleased me,
Fed my duck under yonder tree.

Duck went

slish - y,   slosh - y,

Hen went chipsy, chopsy,
Cat went fiddle-i-fee, fiddle-i-fee.

32

4. Bought me a goose, goose pleased me,
Fed my goose under yonder tree.

Goose went

qua,   qua,

Duck went slishy, sloshy,
Hen went chipsy, chopsy,
Cat went fiddle-i-fee, fiddle-i-fee.

5. Bought me a sheep, sheep pleased me,
Fed my sheep under yonder tree.

Sheep went

baa,   baa,

Goose went qua, qua,
Duck went slishy, sloshy,
Hen went chipsy, chopsy,
Cat went fiddle-i-fee, fiddle-i-fee.

This song has two more verses. In verse 6 the farmer buys a cow.
In verse 7 he buys a horse. Make up sounds for these animals.
Sing the whole song.

ANIMAL SONG

Traditional

Al - li - ga - tor, mon - key, an - te - lope, ca - at,

Rat - tle - snake, buf - fa - lo, moun-tain goat, ba - at.

Al - li - ga - tor, mon - key, an - te - lope, cat,

Rat - tle - snake, buf - fa - lo, moun-tain goat, bat.

TRAMPIN'

Spiritual

I HAVE LOST THE CLOSET KEY

Traditional

Tap the rhythm of the song as you sing.

1. I have lost the clos - et key

In my la - dy's gar - den.

I have lost the clos - et key

In my la - dy's gar - den.

2. Help me find the closet key,
In my lady's garden.

3. I have found the closet key,
In my lady's garden.

36

JOHNNY ONE-NOTE

Aden Lewis/Adapted by Phyllis Schafer

What are the notes in Johnny's song?
What are the two new notes that Johnny has
learned? Find all the **re** notes.

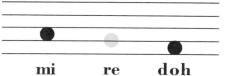

mi   re   doh

John - ny One - Note   now can sing   "Doh-doh - doh-doh - doh - mi -

re - doh."   John - ny feels just like a king   now that he can sing "Mi -

re - doh."   John - ny sings his new notes   ev - 'ry   day,

"Re - re - re,   mi - mi - mi." Yes,   John - ny   One - Note

now   can   sing   "Doh-doh-doh-doh - doh - mi - re - doh."

GET TO BED

Traditional

This song has two parts. One part is repeated. Can you find it?

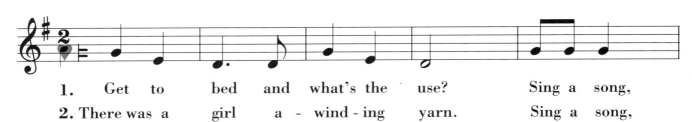

1. Get to bed and what's the use? Sing a song,
2. There was a girl a - wind - ing yarn. Sing a song,

Sal - ly, can't you ki - mi - o. Stick out your feet for a
Sal - ly, can't you ki - mi - o. She wound a ball as ____

chick - en roost. ____ Sing a song, Sal - ly, can't you ki - mi - o.
big as a barn. ____ Sing a song, Sal - ly, can't you ki - mi - o.

Chorus

Old stump, bed pum - mel, cat - nip and pum - me did - dle,

Sing a song, Sal - ly, can't you ki - mi - o.

HUNTER'S COUNTRY

Painting

Ted Harrison

This picture has repeated shapes. Can you find them?

RABBITS

Adapted by Tom Glazer

Chorus

Rab - bits don't have   tails   at   all,   Tails   at   all,   tails   at   all,

Rab - bits don't have   tails   at   all,   Just   wee pow - der   puffs.

(Say) Same song, first verse,
A little bit louder and a little bit worse!

1. Tails are barely there at all,
There at all, there at all,
Tails are barely there at all,
They're not good enough.

Chorus

(Say) Same song, second verse,
A little bit louder and a little bit worse!

2. Ears are longer than their tails,
Than their tails, than their tails,
Ears are longer than their tails,
Just wee bits of fluff.

Chorus

40

SUR LE PONT D'AVIGNON

French Folk Song

Chorus

Sur le pont d'A - vig - non, l'on y dan - se,

l'on y dan - se. Sur le pont d'A - vig - non,

Verse

l'on y dan - se tout en rond. 1. Les de - moi - selles font

comme - ci. Les beaux mes - sieurs font comme - ça.

2. Les poupées font comme-ci,
Les soldats font comme-ça.

MY SHADOW

Diane Shieron

I see my shad-ow, my shad-ow sees me.

When we play to-geth-er we're as hap-py as can be. We

stretch down low to touch our toes, then reach up to the sky. But

when I go in-side to play my shad-ow runs a-way.

42

WINTER

SALLY ON THE SEESAW

Carol King/Adapted by Phyllis Schafer

Sal - ly on the see - saw, Sal - ly on the fence,

Sal - ly get your hair cut fif - teen cents.

SNOW

Gordon M. Fleming

1. Oh, when the snow falls down at night And makes the morn - ing still and white; With not a foot - print you can see, There's no one in the world but me.

2. But then the snowplowman I hear,
He's scraping all the roadways clear.
I must get up; this is the day
When everyone goes out to play.

3. I'll jump into the biggest drift,
Then roll a ball too big to lift,
Then build a fort a metre high
And hide when all the snowballs fly.

OVER THE RIVER AND THROUGH THE WOOD

Traditional Melody/Words by Lydia Maria Child

Crisply

1. O - ver the riv - er and through the wood,

To grand - fa - ther's house we go;

The horse knows the way to car - ry the sleigh

Through the white and drift - ed snow.

O - ver the riv - er and through the wood,

Oh, how the wind does blow! _____

It stings the toes and bites the nose

As o - ver the ground we go. _____

2. Over the river and through the wood,
And straight through the barnyard gate,
We seem to go extremely slow,
It is so hard to wait!
Over the river and through the wood,
Now grandmother's cap I spy!
Hurrah for the fun! Is the pudding done?
Hurrah for the pumpkin pie!

OH, THERE WAS A LITTLE BABY

Alan Mills

Oh, there was a lit - tle Ba - by, Oh my Lord,

Oh, there was a lit - tle Ba - by, Oh my Lord,

Oh, there was a lit - tle Ba - by, Oh my Lord,

way down in Beth - le - hem. Way down in Beth - le - hem.

LITTLE BELLS OF CHRISTMAS

Ann Nichols

Lit - tle bells of Christ - mas -time, ring out loud and clear. _____

Ring out glad tid - ings for Christ - mas is here. To

all the world bring peace, to all the world bring joy. But

most of all bring love _____ to all girls and boys. _____

NOW SING WE ALL MERRILY

Welsh Carol

1. Now sing we all mer-ri-ly, Christ-mas is here,

The day we love best of all days in the year.

2. Bring out the green holly, the fir and the bay,
And deck every cottage for glad Christmas Day.

3. The children are happy, with presents in hand,
From Santa to children all over the land.

THERE IS ST. NICHOLAS

Dutch Folk Song

1. Look, there is the steam - er from far - a - way lands,

It brings us St. Nich - 'las, he's wav - ing his hands.

His horse is a - pranc - ing on deck, up and down,

The ban - ners are wav - ing in vil - lage and town.

2. Black Peter is laughing and tells everyone,
"The good kids get candy, the bad ones get none!"
Oh, please dear St. Nich'las, if Pete and you would
Just visit our house for we all have been good.

LATKES

Music by April Kassirer/Words by Susan Marcus

1. Grate the po - ta - toes for Ha - nuk - kah,

Grate the po - ta - toes for Ha - nuk - kah.

Grate them till they're just like mush!

Take your time, no need to rush!

Take your time, no need to rush!

2. Latkes for Hanukkah,
Latkes for Hanukkah,
Flour, egg and onion too,
Just a pinch of salt will do!
Just a pinch of salt will do!

3. Latkes for Hanukkah,
Latkes for Hanukkah,
Fry them till they're golden brown,
We know they'll be the best in town!
We know they'll be the best in town!

53

CHRISTMAS LULLABY

Richard Gaskell

Hush - a - bye, my lit - tle ba - by, Go to

sleep and do not cry. Hush - a - bye, my lit - tle

ba - by, I will sing a lul - la - by.

There are shepherds on the hillside
Keeping watch o'er their flocks by night.
There's a star up in the heavens
Shining down its wondrous light.

Hushabye, my little baby,
Go to sleep and do not cry.
Hushabye, my little baby,
I will sing a lullaby.

Hear the purring of the kitten
And the cooing of the dove.
Hushabye, my little baby
While I sing to you of love.

Hushabye, my little baby,
Go to sleep and do not cry.
Hushabye, my little baby,

I will sing a lul - la - by.

rit.

I will sing a lul - la - by.

LISTENING:

The Nutcracker

Peter Ilyich Tchaikovsky

After a great feast of sweets, the Sugar Plum Fairy invites Clara and the Prince to enjoy a performance of dances.

Do the Arabian dancers move quickly or slowly?

Listen to the music of the Cossack dancers. Does it move quickly or slowly?

HAPPY NEW YEAR

Ann Nichols

1. Hap - py   New   Year, one, two, three, ___ Hap - py   New   Year.

(clap)   (clap)   Hap - py   New   Year, ev - 'ry - one, the ___

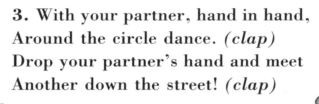

New Year has be - gun! (clap)

2. Let's bring in this great New Year
With singing we can hear. (clap)
Then join hands around the ring,
Let's sing, dance and sing! (clap)

3. With your partner, hand in hand,
Around the circle dance. (clap)
Drop your partner's hand and meet
Another down the street! (clap)

Do you know these songs?

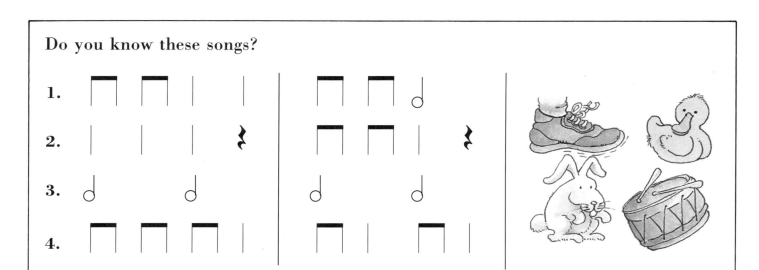

1.
2.
3.
4.

DOCTOR KNICKERBOCKER

Traditional

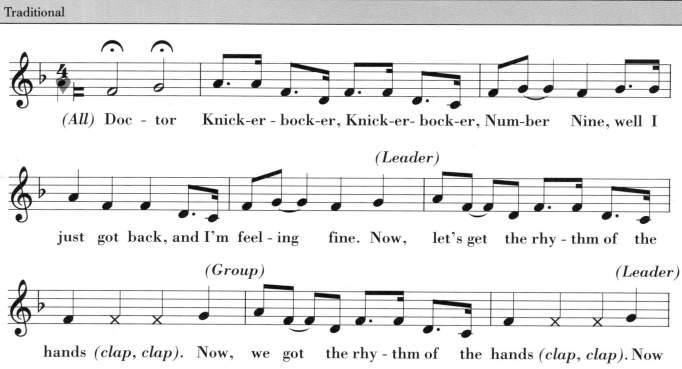

(All) Doc - tor Knick-er - bock-er, Knick-er- bock-er, Num-ber Nine, well I

(Leader)

just got back, and I'm feel-ing fine. Now, let's get the rhy - thm of the

(Group)   *(Leader)*

hands *(clap, clap)*. Now, we got the rhy - thm of the hands *(clap, clap)*. Now

let's get the rhy - thm of the feet *(stamp, stamp)*. Now, we got the rhy - thm of the

(Leader)

feet *(stamp, stamp)*. Now, let's get the rhy - thm of the eyes. ——— Now

(Leader)

we got the rhy - thm of the eyes. ——— Now, let's get the rhy - thm of the

(Group)

hips, *whoo - ee.* Now, we got the rhy - thm of the hips, *whoo - ee.* Now,

we got the rhy - thm of the Num - ber Nine! One, two, three, four,

five, six, sev - en, eight, Nine!

61

HALLELU

Hebrew Folk Song/Translated and Adapted by Judith K. Eisenstein

Tap the accented beats.

Phrase 1

Phrase 2

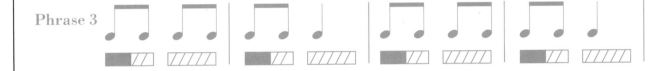

Phrase 3

Phrase 4

Play the accented beat for phrases 1, 2 and 4.

Play the accented beat for phrase 3.

Hal - le - lu - jah,   hal - le - lu - jah,   hal - le - lu - jah,   hal - le - lu!

Hal - le - lu - jah,   hal - le - lu - jah,   hal - le - lu - jah,   hal - le - lu!

Hal - le - lu - jah,   hal - le - lu,   hal - le - lu - jah,   hal - le - lu!

Hal - le - lu - jah,   hal - le - lu - jah,   hal - le - lu - jah,   hal - le - lu!

OKKITOKKIUNGA

Camp Song

Tap the beats as you chant. Where are the strong beats?

Okki - tokki - un - ga,   Okki - tokki - un - ga,

Eh   missa   day   missa   doa   missa   day.   𝄾

(Go back to the beginning)

Hex   -   a   cola   missa   wa_____ ta, _____

  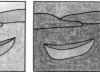

Hex   -   a   cola   missa   wa_____ ta, _____

Okki - tokki - un - ga,   Okki - tokki - un - ga,

Eh   missa   day   missa   doa   missa   day.   𝄾

Ok - ki - to - ki - un - ga,   Ok - ki - to - ki - un - ga,

Eh mis - sa   day mis - sa   do - a mis - sa   day.

(Go back to the beginning)

Hex - a co - la mis - sa   wa———— ta, ————

Hex - a co - la mis - sa   wa ———— ta, ————

Ok - ki - to - ki - un - ga,   Ok - ki - to - ki - un - ga,

Eh mis - sa   day mis - sa   do - a mis - sa   day.

H-A-DOUBLE P-I-N-E-DOUBLE S

Doug Nichol

This song has two parts, A and B. We sing part A first, then we sing part B. When we have finished singing both parts, we sing part A again. We say that this song has an ABA pattern.

A

H - A - dou - ble P - I - N - E - dou - ble S,

H - A - dou - ble P - I - N - E - dou - ble. S.

B

Hap - pi - ness is what we want for ev - ery - one in the

world. Hap - pi - ness we'll try to make for

ev - ery boy and girl, And it's spelled

A

H - A - dou - ble P - I - N - E - dou - ble S,

H - A - dou - ble P - I - N - E - dou - ble S.

LISTENING:

"Ethnic Medley"

Traditional

A

B Tap the beats as you listen. Which beats are stronger?

Continue tapping the beats to the end of this part.

A

CIRCLE ROUND THE ZERO

Game Song Collected by Maureen Kenney

Cir - cle round the Ze - ro, find your lov - in' Ze - ro.

Back, back, Ze - ro, side, side, Ze - ro,

Front, front, Ze - ro, tap your lov - in' Ze - ro.

ROLL ON THE GROUND

American Folk Song

Play a tempo game.

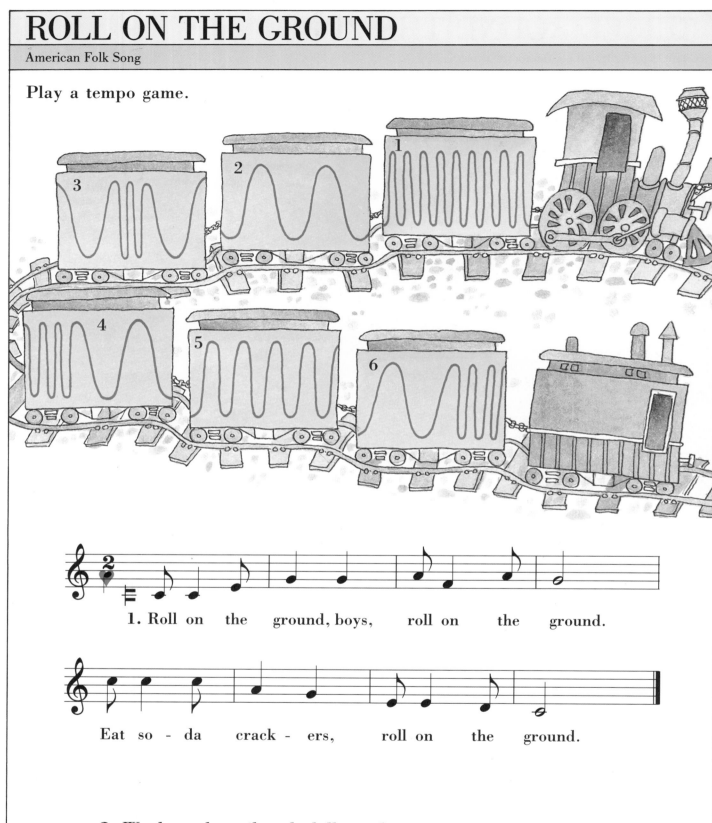

1. Roll on the ground, boys, roll on the ground.

Eat so - da crack - ers, roll on the ground.

2. Work on the railroad, dollar a day.
Eat soda crackers, then shout "Hooray!"

SPECIAL FRIENDS

Adapted by Donna Otto

Friends are spe - cial, friends are true. It's

great to be such a good friend like you.

MAKING VALENTINES

Lee Brodeur

1. I made a fun-ny val-en tine, it is from me to you. I

made some oth-ers too for all my friends at school. So

Chorus

Here's a red, red val-en-tine spe-cial-ly for

you. I hope I'll get one too, 'cause I love you.

2. My favourite one is red and white,
It's for my mom and dad.
I worked at it so long
I know they will be glad. So...

Chorus

VALENTINE RAP

Sandra Geddes and Jeff Adams

I wanted to make a valentine for you,
So I asked my mom exactly what to do.
She said, "My sweet child, you will never go wrong if you
Make it from the heart. Now run along!"

I ran into my room and I looked around but
There wasn't a piece of paper to be found.
So I grabbed my cleanest shirt and my red felt pen and
I started to write this rap to my friend.

Chorus

If I saw a tire-flattened frog, I'd show *you* first,
And if your sister wrecked your new blue kazoo
I'd cry till I'd burst.
For you are my friend, the best one that I know.
Thank you for knowing just how to show me what a good
Friend should be!

I went back to my mom and I showed her the shirt.
She said, "Sandra Ann, how dare you ruin that shirt!
Here's a piece of paper; next time ask for one, please,"
So I sat by the window and looked out at the trees.

The next thing I knew
My mom handed me
The best set of crayons I'd ever seen.
We sat together and made for you
A valentine that was the best we could do.
And it said...

Chorus

This is the end of my rap for you,
If you'll be my valentine, I'll be yours too!

THE CAT

Music by Ronald Lo Presti/Words by Barbara Andress

Why - a - mese are Si - a - mese so sly - a - mese?

They sneak and creep; then sud - den - ly they leap!

74

THREE LITTLE KITTENS

Traditional

1. Three lit - tle kit - tens they lost their mit - tens, And they be - gan to

cry, _____ "Oh, Moth - er dear! We sad - ly fear, Our

mit - tens we have lost." _____ "What! Lost your mit - tens, you

naugh - ty kit - tens, Then you shall have no pie." _____

Chorus

Me - ow, me - ow, me - ow, meow. _____

2. Three little kittens they found their mittens,
And they began to cry,
"Oh, Mother dear! See here, see here,
Our mittens we have found."
"What! Found your mittens,
You lovely kittens,
Then you shall have some pie."

DON GATO

Mexican Folk Song/Translated by David Hoyt

1. Oh, señ - or Don Ga - to was a cat. ——— On a
high red roof Don Ga - to sat. ——— It was there he read a
let - ter, meow, meow, meow, For it made him feel much bet - ter, meow, meow,
meow, As he dreamed a - bout his wed - ding. ———

2. To a white and pretty lady cat,
She was oh so sweet and nice and fat.
There was not a finer kitty, meow, meow, meow,
In the houses of the city, meow, meow, meow,
And he loved her oh so dearly.

3. Then Don Gato in his happiness
Tumbled off the roof; oh what a mess.
Broke his ribs and all his whiskers, meow, meow, meow,
And his little feline haunches, meow, meow, meow.
"¡Ay carramba!" cried Don Gato.

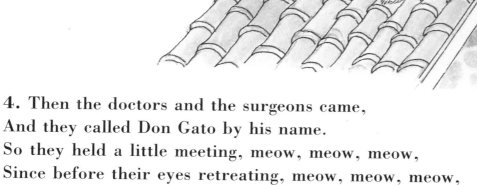

4. Then the doctors and the surgeons came,
And they called Don Gato by his name.
So they held a little meeting, meow, meow, meow,
Since before their eyes retreating, meow, meow, meow,
Was the life of poor Don Gato.

5. But although they tried the livelong day,
Poor Don Gato slowly slipped away.
Oh, it wasn't very pretty, meow, meow, meow,
All the people cried in pity, meow, meow, meow,
At the funeral of Don Gato.

6. The parade passed slowly through the square
Where the smell of fish was everywhere.
The sardines gave such aroma, meow, meow, meow,
He jumped right up from his coma, meow, meow, meow,
He came back to life, Don Gato, *¡Olé!*

TWO LITTLE KITTENS

Collected by Helen Creighton

1. Two little kittens, one stormy night,
    Began to quarrel and then to fight.
    One had a mouse and the other had none,
    That's the way the quarrel had begun.

f "I'll have that mouse," said the little one.

"You'll not have that mouse," said the biggest one.

2.

accel. Then the old woman came out with a broom—
Swept the two little kittens right out of the room.

rit. Poor little kittens had nowhere to go,
Only to lie outside the door.

p Poor little kittens had nowhere to go,
Only to lie outside the door.

3.

pp Then they crept in as quiet as mice,
All wet with snow and cold as ice.
Thinking 'twas better on such a cold night
To lie and sleep than to quarrel and fight.

f Thinking 'twas better on such a cold night
To lie and sleep than to quarrel and fight.

BUT THE CAT CAME BACK

Josef Marais

1. Fred - die Wil - son had a cat that he did - n't want to keep.

He of - fered him for free and he tried to sell him cheap.

He called up - on the preach - er one Sun - day for ad - vice;

The preach - er said, "Yes, leave him here, it would be so nice!"

Chorus

But the   cat came back,   he would-n't stay a - way,

He was sit - ting on the porch on the ver - y next day.

The   cat came back,   he did - n't want to   roam,

The   ver - y next day it   was   home, sweet   home.

KITTY ROCK

Music by Art Barduhn/Words by Al Gilbert

I am a kit - ty and I love to rock. Rock and rock and

rock and rock I am a kit - ty and I love to roll.

Roll and roll and roll and roll. When I rock from

side to side, my lit - tle tail has a groov - y ride.

When I roll I try to show that I can real - ly

go, go, go. I am a kit - ty and I love to bounce.

Bounce and bounce and bounce and bounce. I am a kit - ty and I

love to shake. Shake and shake and shake and shake.

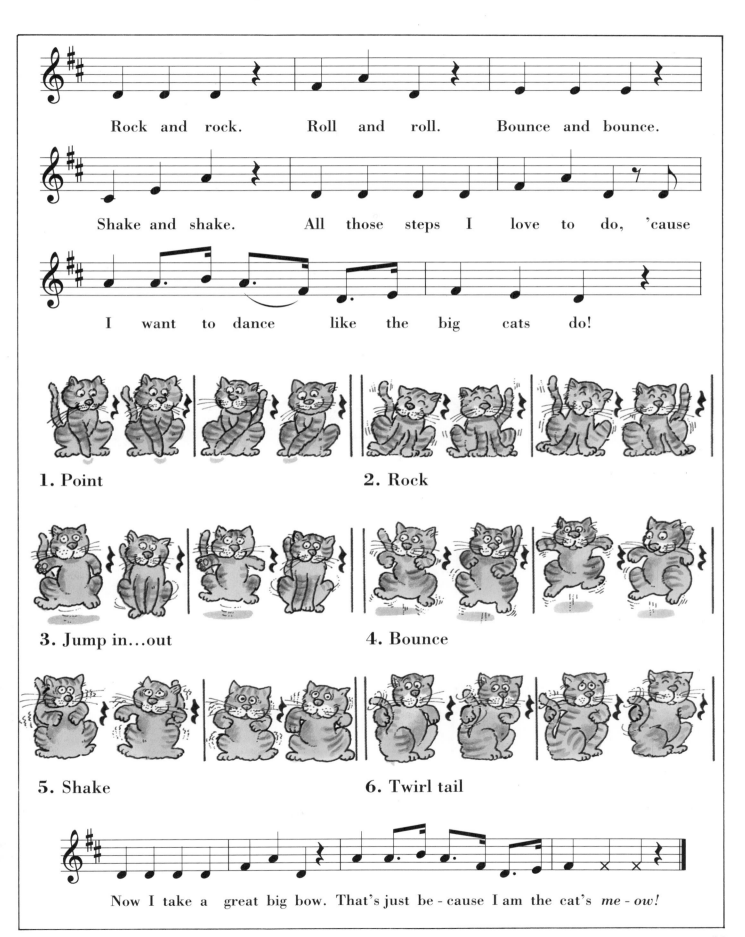

Rock and rock. Roll and roll. Bounce and bounce.

Shake and shake. All those steps I love to do, 'cause

I want to dance like the big cats do!

1. Point

2. Rock

3. Jump in...out

4. Bounce

5. Shake

6. Twirl tail

Now I take a great big bow. That's just be-cause I am the cat's *me-ow!*

THE KANGAROO

Robert J. de Frece

With a short stac - ca - to hop jumps the kan - ga - roo.

From her pouch her ba - by peeks, smi - ling out at you.

TIDE ROLLING IN

Herb Rothgarber

𝄽 𝄽 = ▭ Half Rest

Doh re mi soh   lah.   Lah soh mi re   doh.

Tide roll- ing in,   tide roll - ing out,   bring my lit - tle ship   home.

Bring me safe - ly home, bring me safe - ly home, bring my lit - tle ship   home.

CALYPSO SONG

Herb Rothgarber

How many two-beat rests can you find?

If you ev - er are in the town of Kings - ton on the

is - land of Ja - mai - ca, look up a friend of mine, John - ny is his name.

SAILING

Lois I. Fallis

1. I pad - dle my can - oe but the wind blows my sail - boat,

What a love - ly feel - ing to fly with the wind.

Chorus

Oo _____ oo, _____ oo _____ oo.

2. I have a pair of oars
When I row in my rowboat,
But what a lovely feeling
To fly with the wind.

3. I can steer a boat
When the motor is whirring,
But what a lovely feeling
To fly with the wind.

THE TRAIN FROM ALMENDRAL

Uruguayan Game Song

On the   long rail of   i - ron, the   train from Al - men - dral

Goes a - puff - ing   down   the   trail, With a

Chee - kee, chee - kee   cha,   Chee - kee, chee - kee   cha.

Chee - kee, chee - kee   cha,   Chee - kee, chee - kee   cha.

Find the sound that the train makes. Use these two bells:

88

LISTENING:

"Little Train of Caipira"

Heitor Villa-Lobos

THE SONG OF THE ENGINE

Poem

H. Worsley-Benison

1. (Slowly)

With snort and pant the engine dragged
　　Its heavy train uphill,
And puffed these words the while she puffed
　　And laboured with a will:

2. (Very slowly)

"I think — I can — I think — I can,
　　I've got — to reach — the top.
I'm sure — I can — I will — get there,
　　I sim - ply must — not stop!"

3. (More quickly)

At last the top was reached and passed,
　　And then—how changed the song!
The wheels all joined in the engine's joy,
　　As quickly she tore along!

4. (Very fast)

"I knew I could do it, I knew I could win,
　　Oh, rickety rackety rack!
And now for a roaring rushing race
　　On my smooth and shining track!"

YUMMY YUM YUM

Stella Tossell

1. What do you like for break - fast best?   Meat - balls and spa - ghet - ti.

What lunch is bet - ter than all the rest?   Meat- balls and spa - ghet - ti.

Have some! Yum - my yum yum!   It's   so scrump - tious in   my   tum!

What   do you serve a spe - cial guest?   Meat - balls and spa - ghet - ti.

2. What do you like for a midnight snack? __ __ __ __ ‾‾ ‾‾ ‾‾

When you go on a picnic, what do you pack? __ __ __ __ ‾‾ ‾‾ ‾‾

Have some! Yummy yum yum! It's so scrumptious in my tum!

What makes your lips go smack, smack, smack? __ __ __ __ ‾‾ ‾‾ ‾‾

3. What kind of supper makes you drool? __ __ __ __ ‾‾ ‾‾ ‾‾

What do you take for lunch at school? __ __ __ __ ‾‾ ‾‾

Have some! Yummy yum yum! It's so scrumptious in my tum!

What do they eat in Istanbul? __ __ __ __ ‾‾ ‾‾

SMACK YUM

93

MUSIC MAN

Adapted by Paul Hann

Find the instruments the Music Man plays. How is each instrument played?

I am the Music Man,
I came from down your way,
And I can play...

What can you play? —

Well, I can play on the piano.

I SHALL WAIT AND WAIT

Poem

Alootook Ipellie

As I stand alone on the middle of the ice,
the sky above gets darker by the minute.
The seal has not yet come.
It must be somewhere out there where I cannot see it.
It must be playing in the water below the ice,
or searching for food as I am doing now.
He has his life too, as I do.

I came here to bring food to my family,
so it is most important I stay and wait.
Wait till the seal comes up to the hole below me.
A hole that is filled with salted water.
Food is waiting there.

I shall wait and wait until it comes.

AN ESKIMO LULLABY

Traditional/Collected by Edith Fowke

Still now and hear my sing - ing,

Sleep through the night my dar - ling.

We have a ti - ny daugh - ter,

She is a gift we're giv - en.

Though she as yet knows noth - ing,

She is so sweet I'm sing - ing.

SPRING

THE PERCUSSION FAMILY

The drum is a member of the Percussion Family.
You play percussion instruments by striking, shaking or scraping them.
Can you name the percussion instruments on this page?

THE BRASS FAMILY

These instruments belong to the Brass Family.
Three of them are heard in the song "Oompah-Pah-Pah,"
on the next page. Can you name them?

One of these instruments is *not* heard in the song.
It is called the French horn. Can you find it?

OOMPAH-PAH-PAH

Lee and Sandy Paley

Chorus

Oom - pah pah pah pah,   oom - pah pah pah pah, oom - pah   pah pah pah

pah. _____   Oom - pah pah pah pah,   oom - pah pah pah pah,

oom - pah pah pah pah   pah.   1. I'll play the bass drum, boom! boom! boom!

I'll play   the   bass drum, boom! boom! boom!   I'll play the bass drum,

boom! boom! boom!   Oom - pah pah pah pah   pah. _____

2. I'll play the trombone…

3. I'll play the tuba…

4. I'll play the trumpet…

102

ALPHABET SONG

Traditional

A B C D E F G, H I J K L M N O P.

Q R S, T U V, W— X and Y and Z.

Now I know my A B C's. Tell me what you think of me.

These are repeat signs: $\|\!:$ $:\!\|$ They tell us to repeat the melody between the signs.

Find the melody that is between repeat signs. Sing this melody twice.

A B C D E F G, H I J K L M N O P.

Q R S, T U V, W—— X and Y and Z.

Now I know my A B C's ; tell me what you think of me.

CHARLIE OVER THE OCEAN

Playground Game

Find the repeat signs ||: :|| in this song.

Charlie: Char - lie   o - ver   the   o - cean,
Group: Char - lie   o - ver   the   o - cean,

Charlie: Char - lie   o - ver   the   sea. _____
Group: Char - lie   o - ver   the   sea. _____

Charlie: Char - lie   caught   a   black - bird.
Group: Char - lie   caught   a   black - bird.

Charlie: Can't   catch   me! ____
Group: Can't   catch   me! ____

THE TREE IN THE WOOD

English Folk Song

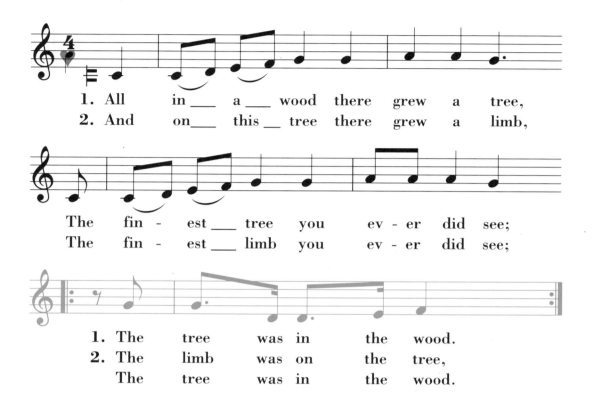

1. All in a wood there grew a tree,
2. And on this tree there grew a limb,

The fin - est tree you ev - er did see;
The fin - est limb you ev - er did see;

1. The tree was in the wood.
2. The limb was on the tree,
   The tree was in the wood.

Chorus

And the green leaves grew all a - round, a - round, a - round,

And the green leaves grew all a - round. _____

3. And on this limb there was a branch…

4. And on this branch there was a nest…

5. And in this nest there was an egg…

6. And in this egg there was a bird…

7. And on this bird there was a wing…

HAYRIDE

Music by April Kassirer/Words by Susan Marcus and April Kassirer

1. Pile the hay___ on the wag - on, oh go - in' on a coun - try

hay - ride. Ev - 'ry - bo - dy read - y? Here we go! ___

Chorus

Go - in' on a coun - try hay - ride. Wig - gle and a wog - gle and a

jig - gle and a jog - gle and an up! down! hay - ride.

2. Like it fast, like it slow,
Goin' on a country hayride.
If you don't like bumps,
Better not go,
Goin' on a country hayride.

3. Grab an apple from the tree,
Goin' on a country hayride.
Bite for you, a bite for me,
Goin' on a country hayride.

4. What'll we do when the hayride ends?
Goin' on a country hayride.
Hop back on and go again,
Goin' on a country hayride.

LISTENING:

"Skater's Waltz"

Emil Waldtenfel

Feel the strong beats as you listen.

SEESAW SACRADOWN (2)

Traditional

LISTENING

"Visions of Sleep"

Lebieg

Tap the hearts as you listen to the music.

Melody 1

Continue tapping the beat.

Melody 2

Continue tapping the beat.

GRETEL, PASTETEL

German Folk Song

5 5 5   6 6 6   5 5

te - tel, oh   where is your   goose? She

3 =   1 1 1

Gre - tel, Pas-

4 4 4   3 3 3   2 2 2   1

sits on the   wa - ter, oh   who turned her   loose?

2. Gretel, Pastetel, oh where is your hen?
She sits on her nest and lays eggs when she can.

3. Gretel, Pastetel, oh where is your cow?
She stays in her stall but I can't milk her now.

Let's tune up.

OJIBWAY SONG

Traditional

Mu - je mu - ke - sin au yaw - yon, Mu - je mu - ke - sin au yaw - yon,

Mu - je mu - ke - sin au yaw - yon, Mu - je mu - ke - sin au yaw - yon.

Worn out are my shoes of deerskin,
Worn out are my shoes of deerskin,
Worn out are my shoes of deerskin,
Worn out are my shoes of deerskin.

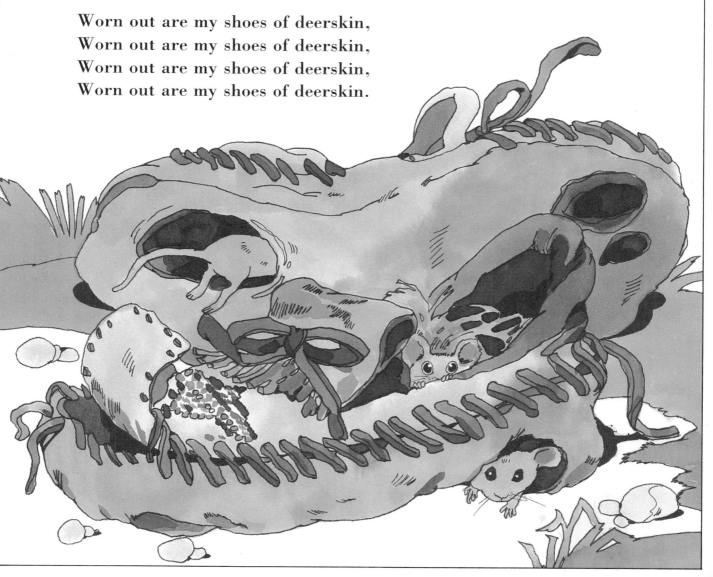

MY NEW GAME

David Hoyt

My new game is nev - er slow. Words and rhy-thm, don't you know.

If you mum-ble out you go. Keep it in time, on with the show!

1.

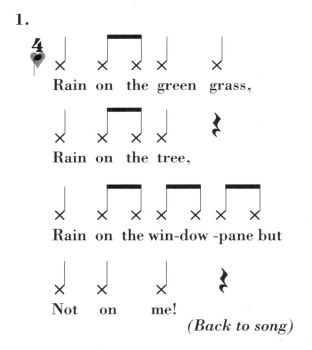

Rain on the green grass,

Rain on the tree,

Rain on the win-dow -pane but

Not on me!

(Back to song)

2.

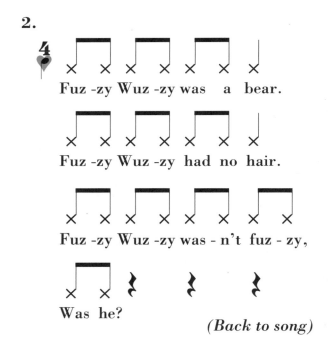

Fuz -zy Wuz -zy was a bear.

Fuz -zy Wuz -zy had no hair.

Fuz -zy Wuz -zy was - n't fuz - zy,

Was he?

(Back to song)

COUNTRY DANCE

Donna Otto

I'm gon - na clap three times, — one, two,

three. I'm gon - na do - si - do, just fol - low __

me! I'm gon - na swing my pal and call YA - HOO!

That's how the coun - try dance goes! _____

MY LITTLE PONY NEEDS NEW SHOES

Traditional

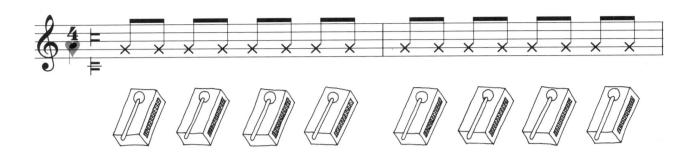

My lit - tle po - ny needs new shoes. How man - y nails must I use?

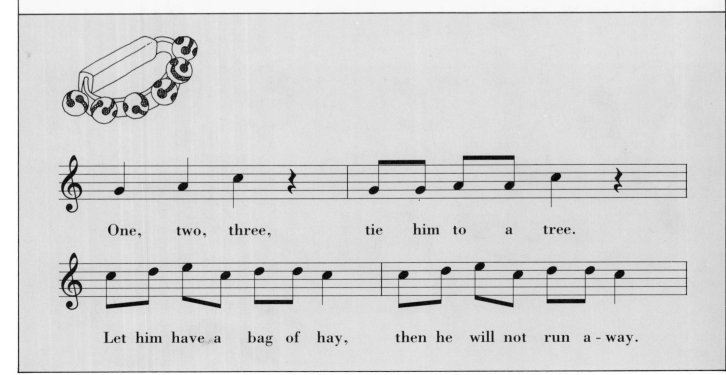

One, two, three, tie him to a tree.

Let him have a bag of hay, then he will not run a - way.

My lit-tle po-ny needs new shoes. How man-y nails must I use?

RIDIN' ALONG SINGING A COWBOY SONG

Margaret I. Fletcher and Margaret C. Denison

Introduction

Rid-in' a - long sing-ing a cow-boy song, Rid-in' a - long sing-ing a song.

Chorus

O - lee - o - lee, o - lee - o - lay, o - lee - o - lay.

Verse

1. My boots are made of leath - er and I wear a cow - boy hat.

I've got my hol - ster tied down and I have a lar - i - at.

I climb in - to the sad - dle and I start out on the trail,

O - lee - o - lay.

2. My pony is a beauty,
His name is Buckaroo.
Whatever I may ask him,
He will know just what to do.
He'll canter oh so slowly
Or he'll gallop like the wind,
O-lee-o-lay.

IT WAS A MOUSE

Nova Scotia Ballad

1. It was a mouse lived in a well - a - hum. There

was a mouse lived in a well And there he lived there ver - y well.

Chorus

And lick - ed - y too de fall de dey, Whack fall de dum.

2. Next came in it was a flea-a-hum.
Next came in it was a flea,
And he fetched in a load of tea.

3. Next came in it was a fly-a-hum.
Next came in it was a fly,
He ate so much it made him die.

4. Next came in it was a tick-a-hum.
Next came in it was a tick,
He ate so much it made him sick.

THE ANIMAL PARADE

Phyllis Schafer

Down the street the animals come,   marching proudly to the drum.

walk   *walk*   *walk*   *walk*   *walk*   *walk*   *walk*   *walk*

Elephant and the grizzly bear   slowly walk with stately air.

slow   *walk*   *slow*   *walk*

Tortoise still the slowest of all,   saunters with a lazy crawl.

very slowly   *very slowly*

Prai - rie dogs and mice must run to   keep in time with eve-ry - one.

run run *run run* *run run* *run run*   *run run* *run run* *run run* *run run*

Horses   as they strut on by   hold their heads and knees up high.

SLUMBER BELLS

Traditional Basque Melody/Adapted by Phyllis Schafer

o = 4 beats

Ding, dong, ding dong ding.

Lit - tle bells will be - gin to ring.

Chil - dren soon will be slum - ber - ing.

Ding, dong, ding dong ding.

THE HAPPY RIVER

French Folk Song

Find the four-beat note.

Hear the hap - py riv - er sing - ing, sing - ing,

Hear the hap - py riv - er sing - ing as it flows.

126

THE BEE

Marjorie P. Hunter

"Zoom," went the bee as he buzzed a - round, buzzed a - round,

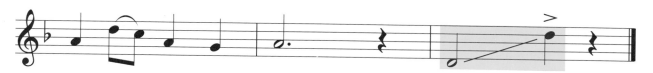

buzzed a - round. "Zoom," went the bee as he buzzed a - round and

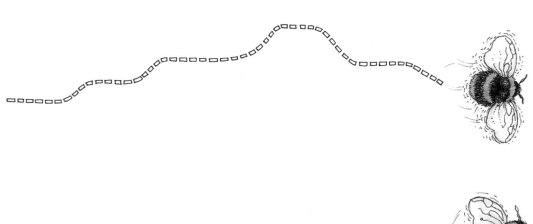

'round, a - round and 'round. "Zoom."____

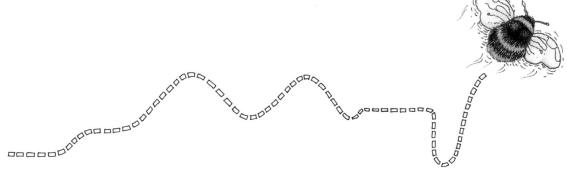

DONNER LE BONJOUR

French Folk Song

Le chat à la pro - me - na - de Doit don - ner le bon -

jour; _____ Le chat à la pro - me - na - de Doit

don - ner le bon - jour. Miaou, miaou, miaou, miaou,

Voi - là ce qu'il dit, il dit: Miaou, miaou,

Miaou, miaou, Voi - là ce qu'il dit.

2. Le chien à la promenade,
Doit donner le bonjour. (*repeat*)
Ouaou! ouaou! ouaou! ouaou!
Voilà ce qu'il dit, il dit:
Ouaou! ouaou! ouaou! ouaou!
Voilà ce qu'il dit.

3. La vache à la promenade,
Doit donner le bonjour. (*repeat*)
Mou-ou, mou-ou, mou-ou, mou-ou,
Voilà ce qu'elle dit, elle dit:
Mou-ou, mou-ou, mou-ou, mou-ou,
Voilà ce qu'elle dit.

TICK TOCK

Traditional German Song

Big   clocks   mark time slow - ly,   tick - tock,   tick - tock.

Small   clocks   mark time fast - er,   tick - tock, tick - tock,

tick - tock, tick - tock. And   the   lit - tle   watch - es mark time

tick - y tock - y, tick - y tock - y   tick - y tock - y tock.

Choose instruments to play the sounds of the big clocks,
the small clocks and the little watches.

LITTLE BLACK ENGINE

Miriam Ulrich

The lit - tle black en - gine goes puff - ing up the

track, _____ Click - e - ty clack, click - e - ty clack, click - e - ty clack,

clack: ___ And as it puffs a - long it sings a fun - ny

song, ___ "Choo - choo, toot - toot, ding - dong." ___

NINESTOSIN

Cree Powwow Song

1. Nin - es - to - sin, Nin - es - to - sin, ko - no ko - no te -

ki - we - yan. Nin - es - to - sin, —— Wa hi ya hi —— ya

hi ya ho, Wa hi ya hi —— ya hi ya ho.

2. Niwikiwan kinis'tohtawin
Niwikiwan kipetawin.
Niwikiwan,
Wa hi ya hi ya hi ya ho,
Wa hi ya hi ya hi ya ho.

3. Niwikiwan nitsimohsis
Kawi n'towmetowananow.
Tamotsikan kisasteki,
Wa hi ya hi ya hi ya ho,
Wa hi ya hi ya hi ya ho.

CANADA OUR HOME

O CANADA

Music by A.C. Lavalée/English Words by R.S. Weir/French Words by A. Routhier

O Can - a - da! Our home and na - tive land,

True pa - triot love in all thy sons com - mand.

With __ glow - ing hearts we __ see thee rise, The __

true North, strong and free; From __ far and wide, O __

Can - a - da, we stand on guard _ for __ thee.

Et ta va - leur, de foi tremp - ée,

Pro - té - ge - ra nos foy - ers et nos droits,

Pro - té - ge - ra nos foy - ers et nos droits.

ACKNOWLEDGEMENTS

Care has been executed to trace ownership of copyright material contained in this text. The publishers will gladly receive information that will enable them to rectify any reference or credits in subsequent editions.

Pg. 5 JOSIE DANCE Adapted from the traditional by Jos Wuytack. Pg. 9 LISTEN TO THE WATER. Lyrics and music by Bob Schneider. © 1980 Schorn Publishing Inc. (PRO Canada) All Rights Reserved. Pg. 15 THANKS A LOT (Raffi) © Copyright 1980 Homeland Publishing (CAPAC), a division of Troubadour Records Ltd. Used by permission. From the album *Baby Beluga* (Raffi). Pg. 20 GRAND OLD DUKE OF YORK Reprinted with the permission of Maureen Raffey and Bernard Lodge from *The Grand Old Duke of York* and The Bodley Head Ltd. Pg. 22 THIS IS HALLOWE'EN by Dorothy Brown Thompson. Pg. 24 STRANGE HALLOWE'EN from *Exploring Music Two* by Eunice Boardman and Beth Landis. Copyright © 1975 by Holt, Rinehart and Winston, Inc. Reprinted by permission of the publisher. Pg. 26 THREE LITTLE FISHES (ITTY BITTY POO) Words and music by Saxie Dowell. © 1939 Chappell & Co. Copyright Renewed. All Rights Reserved. Used by permission. Pg. 30 PAW PAW PATCH From *Exploring Music Two* by Eunice Boardman and Beth Landis. Copyright © 1975 by Holt, Rinehart and Winston, Inc. Reprinted by permission of the publisher. Pg. 37 JOHNNY ONE NOTE NOW CAN SING Words and music by Aden Lewis. Taken from *Listen Look and Sing*, Silver Burdett Co., Morristown, N.J. Adapted by Phyllis Schafer. Pg. 39 HUNTER'S COUNTRY Illustration reprinted by the kind permission of Ted Harrison. Pg. 40 RABBITS (RABBIT AIN'T GOT) Adapted by Tom Glazer. From *Eye Winker, Tom Tinker, Chin Chopper-50 Musical Fingerplays* by Tom Glazer. Doubleday & Co., New York. © Songs Music, Inc., Scarborough, N. Y. 10510. By permission. Pg. 42 MY SHADOW Words and music by Diane Shieron. Used by permission. Pg. 44 SALLY ON THE SEESAW Words and music by Carol King. *RECORDER ROUTES I* © Memphis Musicraft Publ., 3149 Southern Ave., Memphis, TN 38111. Pg. 45 SNOW Words and music by Gordon Fleming. Reprinted with the kind permission of Leslie Music Supply. Pg. 46 OVER THE RIVER AND THROUGH THE WOOD Words by Lydia Maria Child, music traditional. Pg. 48 OH, THERE WAS A LITTLE BABY by Alan Mills, Reprinted with the kind permission of the estate of Alan Mills. Pg. 49 LITTLE BELLS OF CHRISTMAS by A. Nichols. Pg. 52 LATKES Music and lyrics by April and Susan from the recording *Homefree!* Pg. 54 CHRISTMAS LULLABY Words and music by Richard Gaskell. Pg. 58 HAPPY NEW YEAR by A. Nichols. Pg. 60 DOCTOR KNICKERBOCKER Reprinted with the permission of McGraw-Hill Ryerson Ltd. Pg. 62 HALLELU Hebrew folk song translated and adapted by Judith K. Eisenstein. Copyright © 1938 and renewed copyright © 1966 by Judith K. Eisenstein. Reprinted by permission of the author. Pg. 66 H-A-DOUBLE P-I-N-E-DOUBLE S Words and music by Doug Nichol. Copyright © 1975 by Doug Nichol. Reprinted by permission. Pg. 69 CIRCLE ROUND THE ZERO Game song collected by Maureen Kenney, Colrain MA. © Maureen Kenney. Pg. 70 ROLL ON THE GROUND From *Holt Music, Grade Two*. Copyright © 1988 by Holt, Rinehart and Winston, Inc. Reprinted by permission of the publisher. Pg. 71 SPECIAL FRIENDS Adapted by Donna Otto. © 1984 Jenson Publications, Inc. International Copyright Secured. *MADE IN U.S.A.* All Rights Reserved. Used by permission. Pg. 72 MAKING VALENTINES Words and music by Lee Brodeur. Used by permission. Pg. 73 VALENTINE RAP by Sandra Geddes and Jeff Adams. Used by permission. Pg. 74 THE CAT Words by Barbara Andress, music by Robert Lo Presti. From *Holt Music, Grade Two*. Copyright © 1988 by Holt, Rinehart and Winston, Inc. Reprinted by permission of the publisher. Pg. 76 DON GATO Mexican folk song translated by David Hoyt. Used by permission. Pg. 78 TWO LITTLE KITTENS Traditional, collected by Helen Creighton. From *Eight Ethnic Folk Songs for Young Children*. © Copyright by Gordon V. Thompson Music, A Division of Canada Publishing Corporation, Toronto, Canada. Used by permission. Pg. 80 BUT THE CAT CAME BACK Words and music by Josef Marais. Reprinted with the permission of the Fideree Music Company. Pg. 82 KITTY ROCK Lyrics by Al Gilbert, music by Art Barduhn. Pg. 84 THE KANGAROO Words and music by Robert J. de Frece. Used with the permission of the Alfred Publishing Co., Inc. Pg. 85 TIDE ROLLING IN Words and music by Herb Rothgarber. Used with the permission of the Alfred Publishing Co., Inc. Pg. 86 CALYPSO SONG Words and music by Herb Rothgarber. Used with the permission of the Waterloo Music Company. Pg. 91 THE SONG OF THE ENGINE by H. Worsley-Benison. Extract taken from *Round About Six: Poems for Today* by Margaret Rawlins. Reproduced by kind permission of Unwin Hyman Ltd. Pg. 92 YUMMY YUM YUM Written by Stella Tossell. Published by Wickham Music from the LP by Paul Hann *Snyder the Spider*. Pg. 94 MUSIC MAN Traditional song arranged by Paul Hann. Published by Wickham Music. Pg. 96 I SHALL WAIT AND WAIT by Alootook Ipellie. Used by permission. Pg. 98 ESKIMO LULLABY Words and music traditional, collected by Edith Fowke. Reprinted with the kind permission of the Waterloo Music Company Ltd. Pg. 102 OOMPAH-PAH-PAH Words and music by Lee and Sandy Paley. Published by Schoolhouse Corporation. Pg. 108 HAYRIDE Music and Lyrics by April and Susan from the recording *Join In!* Pg. 112 VISIONS OF SLEEP by Lebieg. © 1981 by Hal Leonard Publishing Corporation. International Copyright Secured. All Rights Reserved. Used by permission. Pg. 116 MY NEW GAME Words and music by David Hoyt. Used by permission. Pg. 117 COUNTRY DANCE by Donna Otto. © 1982 Jenson Publications Inc. International Copyright Secured. *MADE IN U.S.A.* All Rights Reserved. Used by permission. Pg. 120 RIDIN' ALONG SINGING A COWBOY SONG Words and music by Margaret I. Fletcher and Margaret C. Denison. © Copyright 1957 by Gordon V. Thompson Music, A Division of Canada Publishing Corporation, Toronto, Canada. Used by permission. Pg. 127 THE BEE Words and music by Marjorie P. Hunter. Pg. 131 LITTLE BLACK ENGINE Words and music by Miriam Ulrich. Pg. 135 O CANADA National Anthem published under authority of the Speaker of the House of Commons, Ottawa, K1A 0A6.

CLASSIFIED INDEX

ALPHABETICAL INDEX